# First World War
### and Army of Occupation
# War Diary
## France, Belgium and Germany

25 DIVISION
7 Infantry Brigade,
Brigade Trench Mortar Battery
1 July 1916 - 28 August 1916

WO95/2244/7

The Naval & Military Press Ltd
www.nmarchive.com
**Published in association with The National Archives**

Published by

## The Naval & Military Press Ltd

Unit 10 Ridgewood Industrial Park,

Uckfield, East Sussex,

TN22 5QE England

Tel: +44 (0) 1825 749494

www.naval-military-press.com

www.nmarchive.com

*This diary has been reprinted in facsimile from the original. Any imperfections are inevitably reproduced and the quality may fall short of modern type and cartographic standards.*

© **Crown Copyright**
**Images reproduced by permission of The National Archives, London, England, 2015.**

# Contents

| Document type | Place/Title | Date From | Date To |
|---|---|---|---|
| Heading | WO95/2244-7 | | |
| Heading | 7th Trench Mortar Bty Jly-Aug 1916 | | |
| Heading | 7th Trench Mortar Battery July 1916 | | |
| War Diary | | 01/07/1916 | 29/07/1916 |
| Heading | 7th Trench Mortar Battery August 1916 | | |
| War Diary | | 01/08/1916 | 28/08/1916 |

25TH DIVISION
7TH INFY BDE

7TH TRENCH MORTAR BTY
JLY - AUG 1916

25TH DIVISION
7TH INFY BDE

7th Inf. Bde.
-----------

25th Division
-----------

7th TRENCH MORTAR BATTERY,

JULY, 1916.

Army Form C. 2118.

L.S. Bty.
7.7 M Batty
Vol I

# WAR DIARY
or
## INTELLIGENCE SUMMARY
(Erase heading not required.)

Instructions regarding War Diaries and Intelligence Summaries are contained in F.S. Regs., Part II. and the Staff Manual respectively. Title Pages will be prepared in manuscript.

| Place | Date | Hour | Summary of Events and Information | Remarks and references to Appendices |
|---|---|---|---|---|
| | 1916 July | | | |
| | 2/7/16 | | Left LABEVILLERS at 9pm & marched to VARENNE | |
| | 3/7/16 | | Left VARENNE at 5pm marched to HEDAUVILLE. Left HEDAUVILLE at 10pm marched to the assembly trenches in AVELUY WOOD. | |
| | 4/7/16 | | The Battery relieved the battery in the trenches in the afternoon. Pte. DITCHFIELD No. 15062. 10th CHESHIRE REGt wounded. Capt. D.W. REID 16th SEAFORTH HDRS, wounded on night of 4/5th. Cpl. CLOUGH. A. No. 15651 8th E.L.N. LANCS, wounded. No. 12354 Pte. CARPENTER killed. 1 gun put out of action by shell fire. | |
| | 5/7/16 | | All in LEIPZIG SALIENT. 4 Guns were put in position in LEIPZIG SALIENT to assist an attack by the 1st WILTSHIRE REGt at 4.30pm. The 4 guns were registered onto the enemy trench which was to be attacked, & fired rapid for half a minute while the 1st WILTSHIRES were going across. 60 rounds were fired during that half minute. Casualties — Lieut. B.C.G. CLARKE 3rd WORCESTER REGt: wounded. No 874 Pte. BUTCHER wounded. | |

Army Form C. 2118.

# WAR DIARY
## or
## INTELLIGENCE SUMMARY
*(Erase heading not required.)*

| Place | Date | Hour | Summary of Events and Information | Remarks and references to Appendices |
|---|---|---|---|---|
| | 6/7/16 | | 7 Guns were placed in the LEIPZIG SALIENT with 150 to 160 on each to assist a second attack by the 1st WILTSHIRE REGT. Casualty. No. 9158 Pte. WHEATLEY A. wounded | |
| | 7/7/16 | At 9.30 A.M. | for 2.30 seconds, while the first WILTSHIRE REGT were going over, all 7 guns fired rapid. 100 rounds were fired. Then all guns lifted to fresh a range & during the day about 600 rounds were fired. Extract from SPECIAL DIVISIONAL ORDER dated 17.7.16. " The work performed by the Harrison with the Trench Mortar Battery was most effective. During the 30 seconds intense bombardment preceding the assault, his guns fired in fact more than 100 rounds with great accuracy, putting out of action an enemy machine gun". Casualties. 2Lt. A.E. HAMPSON 16th CHESHIRE REGT. Killed No 12401 Pte. JOHNSON H. wounded. No. 15089 WOODWARD. J.W. wounded Cpl. No. 14582 PRESTON R. wounded. No. 16935 Pte. DELLEY G. wounded | |

# WAR DIARY
## INTELLIGENCE SUMMARY
*(Erase heading not required.)*

Army Form C. 2118.

| Place | Date | Hour | Summary of Events and Information | Remarks and references to Appendices |
|---|---|---|---|---|
| | 8/7/16 | | The Battery was relieved in the trenches, marched to AVELUY Wood, & at midnight 8/9th marched to bivouacs 1 mile East of ALBERT, arriving at dawn. | |
| | 9th | | On the night of the 9/10th the Battery relieved the 7th L.T.M. Battery in the trenches at LA BOISELLE. Casualty No 22818 Pte SHIPMAN T. wounded. | |
| | 10th | | 2pm. 1 gun was taken up with the 8th LOYAL NORTH LANCASHIRE REGT. to assist in a bombing attack up a communication trench opposite POZIERES. During the attack about 150 rounds were fired on several occasions large groups of the enemy were caught by our Lewis in the open, when the effect was great. Casualty No 26733 Pte Robinson H.J. 10 McINSHIRIS REGT wounded. | |
| | 11th | | | |
| | 12th | | Spent the day getting guns into position. Just 40 rounds onto enemy trench leading to OVILLERS. Casualty No 18870 Pte WORDSLEY. T.B. wounded. | |
| | 13th | | Took a gun & 300 rounds to the advanced trench opposite POZIERES, held by the 3rd WORCESTERS. | |

# Army Form C. 2118.

## WAR DIARY
### or
### INTELLIGENCE SUMMARY
*(Erase heading not required.)*

Instructions regarding War Diaries and Intelligence Summaries are contained in F. S. Regs., Part II. and the Staff Manual respectively. Title Pages will be prepared in manuscript.

| Place | Date | Hour | Summary of Events and Information | Remarks and references to Appendices |
|---|---|---|---|---|
| | 14th | | Put one gun in position to fire into OVILLERS about 40 rounds were fired at night. | |
| | 15th | | The Battery was relieved by the 74th T.M. Battery & went to Bivouacs just outside ALBERT. | |
| | 16th | | Marched to FORCEVILLE. | |
| | 17th | | At FORCEVILLE. | |
| | 18th | | Marched to BEAUVAL starting at 7 p.m. carrying all our transport on 16 hand carts. | |
| | 19th | | At BEAUVAL. | |
| | 20th | | Left BEAUVAL at 2 p.m. marched to Bois de WARNIMONT near AUTHIE arriving at 6 p.m. | |
| | 21st | | At Bois de WARNIMONT. | |
| | 23rd | | Marched to MAILLY. Relieved the 83rd T.M. Battery in the trenches | |
| | 24th & 25th | | Made emplacements in the new support line. | |

Major R.
O.C. 7th T.M.B.

7th Inf. Bde.

25th Division

7th TRENCH MORTAR BATTERY,

AUGUST, 1916.

Army Form C. 2118.

# WAR DIARY
## or
## INTELLIGENCE SUMMARY

(Erase heading not required.)

7th Trench Mortar Battery
Vol 2

| Place | Date | Hour | Summary of Events and Information | Remarks and references to Appendices |
|---|---|---|---|---|
| | 1st Aug '16 Aug. | | In the trenches immediately North of River ANCRE. on the right of the 1/2nd 40 mouths was fired onto an enemy looking post between the railway & river. This was the only firing done during the 6 days. 4 deep trench mortar positions were made in the new support line. | |
| | Aug 6th | | The Battery was relieved by the 18th T.M.B. & marched to BERTRANCOURT (billets). | |
| | Aug 8th | | 2nd Lieut J. KILBY 10th Gloucester Regt. & 2nd Lt F.J.H. HEDGES 10th Gloucester Regt. joined the Battery from the 3rd Worcester Regt. | |
| | Aug 10 | | The Battery moved from BERTRANCOURT to VAUCHELLES & went in bivouacs for the night. | |
| | Aug 11. | | Took over billets in VAUCHELLES | |
| | Aug 13th | | The Battery marched to billets in PUCHEVILLERS. | |
| | Aug 17 | | The Battery marched to HEDAUVILLE billets | |
| | Aug 19 | | The Battery relieved the 146 T.M.B in the LEIPZIG Salient. | |

# WAR DIARY or INTELLIGENCE SUMMARY

Army Form C. 2118.

| Place | Date | Hour | Summary of Events and Information | Remarks and references to Appendices |
|---|---|---|---|---|
| | Aug 21st | | 3 guns placed in the QUARRIES fired about 160 rounds assisting the 1st WILTSHIRE Regt. in their attack on the Rifle Pits R31c96-79. R31c96-86. & immediately after the attack 1 gun with ammunition was brought up & placed at point 90. covering the communication trench. Casualties 2/Lt J. KILBY killed. 2/Lt E.J.H. HEDGES - Shell Shock. | |
| | 24th | | 3 guns from the QUARRIES fired 130 rounds on the trenches attached to the 1st WILTSHIRE Regt. fire zone C. Zone + J. mine & 2 guns fired about 80 rounds on the trenches attached to the 3rd Worcester Regt. at the same time 1 gun was taken forward into the trenches captured by the 1st Wiltshire Regt. & placed behind a landing post at point R31c45. about 100 rounds were fired from this gun during the afternoon & night. | |
| | 25th | | 3 guns were placed to fire on the strong trench R31c46 - R31A42 about 60 rounds were fired on this trench. Casualties No.6769 Pte MITCHELL J.J. wounded No.17400 " Wagstaff. W. " - 12600 " Rathbone. J. " - 36524 " " No.9819 Pte Cross R.J. wounded No.15045 " Ham. H. " | |

| Place | Date | Hour | Summary of Events and Information | Remarks and references to Appendices |
|---|---|---|---|---|
| | Aug 26th | | 3 guns fired 60 rounds rapid to assist the 8th Loyal NORTH LANCASHIRE Regt. in their attack on the trench R.31.c.46 - R.31.A.42. & after the attack on gun fired at intervals on an enemy landing post at point R.31.c.46. | |
| | Aug 27th | | The Battery was relieved by the 75th T.M.B. & marched to HÉDAUVILLE to billets | |
| | Aug 28 | | The Battery marched from HÉDAUVILLE to BOUZINCOURT to billets. | |

Aidan Harrison Capt.
O.C. 7 T.M. Battery

www.ingramcontent.com/pod-product-compliance
Lightning Source LLC
Chambersburg PA
CBHW081253170426
43191CB00037B/2145